# Timeless Elegance

*True Beauty Knows No Age
and Inner Beauty Never Fades*

## C.J. MARIE

*Dedicated to all the women
who share my vision of excellence and beauty
inside and out*

# Books by C.J. Marie

*Timeless Elegance*

*Resolutions*

*Revelations*

*Reflections*

*Words of Wisdom*

*Accents of a Women*

*Captured Thoughts*

*Afterthoughts of Yesterday*

*Legacy of Stable Dreams*

*Shadowed Love*

*Reflections of Time*

*Melody of Love*

*Days of Difference*

## Children's Stories:

*Mi Primer Dia-Escolar*

*My First Day in Kindergarten*

## Chap Books:

*Of Love and Sorrow*

*Fly With Your Dreams*

## Guides:

*Tell Me What to Do*

*Pageant Tips*

# Table of Contents

# Introduction

The foundation of style lies in embracing C. J. Marie's philosophy of living by design. Beauty never fades when you approach life with a positive perspective. Developing your own personal style is a journey that unfolds throughout your life. The mental image you hold of yourself sets the stage for success. Every woman possesses a unique sense of style, and how she projects that image influences the world around her. Women are authentic in their individuality and inspiring them to believe in themselves encourages each to reach their fullest potential.

Honor your journey of self-discovery and style. Engage in self-reflection and dare to look deeply within. At every stage of life, we are continuously changing, evolving, and emerging into the person we are meant to be. By gazing into the mirror of your soul, you will uncover the reflection of transformation and growth period as woman, we are on a quest to live meaningful and purposeful lives. We strive for self-reinvention, constantly searching for the power to pursue our passions. These life changing moments reveal that we are far more capable than we ever imagined.

This realization becomes the catalyst that propels us towards our dream. We are woman of worth, filled with power, confidence, and an irresistible energy that inspires and influences others. By stepping outside of our comfort zones, we challenge ourselves to go further than we thought possible. Finding the courage to take on these challenges unlocks the dreams within our hearts, waiting to be freed.

Live and speak your truth. There is power in your vision and strength in your voice. Embrace and celebrate the unique person you are. There is only one of you, so strive to be the best version of yourself.

# *Timeless Beauty*

**"S** ave the best for last" and "you get better with age" our phrases we've all heard throughout our lives. As a pageant consultant and a multi time state and national queen, my experience in the world of pageantry spans over forty years. From toddlers to senior citizens, the pageant world has evolved to celebrate contestants of all ages, particularly mature women. These remarkable individuals graced the runway with radiance and style, showcasing their unique beauty and maximizing their talents.

Mature women bring a distinct advantage to pageantry, the wisdom and life experience that come with age that they have lived, learned, and grown in ways that younger contestants are still discovering. While youths' innocence has its charm, today's pageants focus on far more than superficial beauty. Television and print media have embraced and celebrated age, giving women the confidence to pursue new opportunities.

There is indeed life after 60, and today's mature woman refused to let age define or limit them. Just look at inspiring figures like Maye Musk at 76, Jackie O'Shaughnessy at 65, and Carmen Dell' Orefice at 93. These women did not let their age dictate their potential - they used it as a platform to achieve their dreams. Their stories remind us that with discipline, focus, resilience, and persuasiveness perseverance, anything is possible. Success comes to those who confront challenges with enthusiasm and unwavering dedication.

Beauty is not bound by age; it is a quality that resides within each of us, making us special and unique. While the definition of beauty may vary across individuals and eras, one truth remains, beauty is timeless. Age fosters wisdom and knowledge, and for many, life truly begins at sixty. It is never too late to challenge yourself and strive to be more than you ever imagined. The period of time waits for no one, and the only limits are those we place on ourselves.

The world of pageantry holds invaluable lessons for life. True beauty radiates from within, reflecting our inner qualities outwardly. Winning pageants and wearing a crown has always been about more than the title. For me, my crowns have served as a purpose, a platform to make a difference in the world. They have been my megaphones, amplifying my voice to inspire and empower women to reach their full potential.

I encourage every woman to embrace and celebrate who she is. Have faith, believe in yourself, and tackle challenges with courage. The best is yet to come, and by giving the best of yourself, you can help make the world a better place. Beauty is timeless, and so is the ability to dream, achieve, then inspire.

*Every woman should live her life with hope, hard work,
possibility, opportunity and anticipation
and believe that she is capable to accomplish anything
she sets out to be*

*Good friends help you find important things
when you have lost them.
Things like your smile, your hope, and your courage*

*Always stand up for what you think is right
even if you are the only one standing*

*No dream is too big no challenge is too great*

– Donald J. Trump

*Peace through strength and chaos through weakness*

— John Radclif

*Today is the oldest you've ever been,*
*yet the youngest you'll ever be*

◆

*If a woman is able to get close to your man,*
*she is not the problem, he is.*
*The fact that another woman feels so welcomed*
*reflects on how your man acts behind your back*

◆

*The prettiest smiles hide the deepest secrets,*
*The prettiest eyes have cried the most tears, and*
*The kindest hearts have felt the most pain*

◆

*Seize every day,*
*it is a chance to become the most beautiful day of your life*

— Ivanka Trump

◆

*I live by one motto that was told to me some time ago. "*
*A vision without action is only a daydream,*
*and tomorrow is promised to no one,"*
*so I have taken the necessary actions to make my dream*
*a reality and encourage women at any age to believe*
*the best is yet to come, celebrate yourself, live in the moment,*
*be the vision you see for yourself.*
*The time is now and there is no time to lose*

— C. J. Marie

*I bent until I broke.*
*But the thing about being strong:*
*you always find a way to get back up and fight harder*

— Ravenwolf

*Don't bother about problems that do not exist,*
*try to ignore issues that do not need your attention,*
*constant worrying is not a solution, it's a problem*
*you need to get out of this constant and perpetual stress made,*
*start to see how beautiful life really is*

— Sangeta Rana

*You can be a badass, strong, confident woman...*
*Who is also soft, maturing, kind and graceful.*
*You can have self-discipline and self-compassion.*
*You can be emotional and tough.*
*You can be everything and anything you want.*
*That is your power*

◆

*Just because you are happy*
*it doesn't mean that the day is perfect*
*but that you have looked beyond its imperfection*

— Bob Marley

◆

*Don't compare yourself to others*
*there is no comparison between the sun and the moon,*
*they shine when it's their time*

◆

*The sand will brush off*
*The salt will wash off*
*The tan will fade away*
*The memories will last a lifetime*

◆

*A sliver of time between those bridges*
*has made us who we are today.*
*For better or worse we own it.*
*Whether it was street smarts learned, or innocence lost.*
*No other generation will reap the knowledge*
*we obtain from Astoria Park in Queens NY*

*If you want something said ask a man,*
*if you want something done ask a woman*

— Margaret Thatcher

*As we grow older, real beauty travels from face to the heart,*
*appeal turns to charm, heart to wisdom*
*and moments to shared memories.*
*The true beauty of life is not how happy you are now*
*but how happy others are because of you*

*Self-discovery is an awakening*

*And one day she discovered that she was fierce and strong and full of life, and that not even she could hold herself back because her passion burned brighter than her flaws*

— Mark Anthony

◆

*She's a deadly combination of wild and fragile, easier to persuade but difficult to conquer*

◆

*Don't let people tell you how to live or how to love, follow your own soul, it knows the way*

◆

*When you come out of the storm, you won't be the same person that walked in. That's what the storm is all about*

◆

*The naked truth is always better then the best dressed lie*

◆

*Nothing matches the feeling of victory*

— C. J. Marie

◆

*I will never accept being treated like an option,*
*when I should be treated like a priority*

— Ravenwolf

*Strength to overcome difficulties*
*comes from having a strong faith*

— C. J. Marie

*Be the hand that reaches out.*
*Be the smile for those who have no reason to smile.*
*Be the light for those who live in darkness*

*Why stop when you can make an impact on a person's life*

# Unspoken Feelings

There are moments when we long to express our feelings but struggle to find the right words or the appropriate circumstances to say them. How often do we replay conversations in our minds, thinking, *I should have said that,* or wondering if our words conveyed the wrong message? Some people use a flurry of words yet say very little, while others speak sparingly but communicate with clarity and impact.

Unspoken feelings often manifest through facial expressions — conveying criticism, fear, or happiness without a single word. These unspoken words become a form of silence. While silence is often said to be golden, true feelings and emotions need to be released. Bottling them up can create barriers in communication, leaving our intentions misunderstood or our needs unfulfilled.

We all have feelings that deserve to be expressed, not only for our own emotional well-being but to foster understanding with those who matter most to us. Communication is the bridge that connects our inner world with others, and finding ways to share our emotions helps to strengthen relationships and create a deeper connection.

*Never worry about being* special *to someone.*
*Being* special *to yourself is what is important*

– C. J. Marie

*You must have imagination to invent or reinvent yourself*

– C. J. Marie

*God must have looked down on me and said:*
*"I think I'll give her sequins and diamonds*
*and make her shine"*
*and he did*

– C. J. Marie

*If life is not challenging for you then change direction*

– C. J. Marie

*I answer to two people in life: myself and God*

– C. J. Marie

*I am* unique and authentic *I
don't know how to be any other way*

— C. J. Marie

*When you really want something bad enough
you find a way to make it happen*

— C. J. Marie

*I am who I am and I don't make any excuses for it*

— C. J. Marie

*If you want to stand out in this world, you have to be different*

— C. J. Marie

*Aging is not lost youth
but a new age of opportunity and strength*

— Betty Friedman

*Helping one person might not change the whole world,*
*but it could change the world for one person*

*Think about a balloon with an imprint of your beautiful face.*
*As each decade of life passes air is released from the balloon*
*and the face begins to wrinkle and begins to shrivel up.*
*Beauty has delicately passed*
*but the wisdom and the beauty of the soul live on*

*If you're going to stand out you might as well be outstanding*

— Vivas

*I love you more today than yesterday and less than tomorrow*

*[In Italian] Ti amo oggi piu de ieri e meno de domani*

*My clothes are my friends they keep old memories alive*

— C. J. Marie

*Look at the moon,*
*Look at the stars,*
*Look at everything that is beautiful*

◆

*[In Italian]*
*Guarda la luna,*
*Guarda la stelle,*
*Guarda tutti le cosi belle*

◆

*Our lives are the sum of our choices*

◆

*Happiness is a choice, not a result.*
*Nothing will make you happy unless you choose to be.*
*No person will make you happy*
*unless you decide to be happy,*
*your happiness will not come to you,*
*it can only come from you*

– Ralph Maeston

◆

*She dances to the songs in her head,*
*She speaks with the rhythm of her heart, and*
*She loves from the depth of her soul*

– Gypsys Angels

*People can destroy your image, damage your personality,*
*create rumors about you.*
*But they can never take away your good deeds,*
*because no matter how they describe you,*
*you will always be admired by those who know you best*

*Life isn't about finding yourself; it's about creating yourself*

*True freedom is understanding that we have a choice*
*in who and what we allow to power over us*

# The Power of Quotes

In a world where a woman's empowerment is an ongoing journey, quotes serve as a guiding light reminding us of the strength and resilience and potential a woman possess.

Quotes inspire us to ensure that a woman's voice is heard, and contributions are not only recognized but valued. Quotes are powerful tools of inspiration in your life. They can motivate you to lend a fresh perspective in your way of thinking which in turn can lead to a transformation in your life.

*Happiness is not by chance but by choice*

Everyone makes mistakes in life,
but that doesn't mean they have to pay for it
for the rest of their life.
Sometimes good people make bad choices,
it doesn't mean they are bad, it just means they are human

*Self-worth comes from one thing: a belief that you're worthy*

— Dr. Wayne Dyer

*If you have to make people know how wonderful you are,*
*you are an extremely weak individual.*
*Those who speak less of themselves stand out more*

— C. J. Marie

*Trust your instincts they are messages from your soul*

*You are a beautiful beacon of light, keep shining. The world
needs your light in this darkened world*

— C. J. Marie

*When I'm good, I'm very good. But when I'm bad, I'm better*

— Mae West

*One of the happiest moments in life is when you find
the courage to let go of what you can't change*

*Imperfection is beauty,
madness is genius,
and it's better to be absolutely ridiculous
than absolutely boring*

— Marilyn Monroe

*Being with no one is better than being with the wrong one.
Sometimes those who fly solo have the strongest wings*

*Reset, restart, refocus as many times as you need.*
*Just don't give up*

— Carlos Dominguez

*They might think they played you, but in reality,*
*they only played themselves out of a decent person*

*Strong women are not simply born,*
*they are made by the storms they walk through*

*Be the beauty in someone's helplessness,*
*be the light, be the color, be the fragrance, be the hope*

— Sangeta Rana

*When you find someone who makes you feel the same way*
*music does, that's when you found someone special*

*Youth is a gift of nature.*
*But age is a work of art and we are a masterpiece*

◆

*Your smile is your logo,*
*your personality is your business card,*
*and the way you make people feel is your trademark*

◆

*True beauty knows no age*

◆

*The truth is sometimes you have to do what's best for you*
*and your life, not what's best for everyone else*

◆

*You are the artist of your own canvas.*
*It's your brush, your color, your design.*
*Never allow anyone to paint your picture*

– C. J. Marie

◆

*If you are searching for that one person*
*who will change your life, look into the mirror*

*Value your worth*

*Life is like a piano.*
*White keys are happy moments,*
*and the black are sad moments.*
*Both keys are played together*
*to give us sweet music called life*

— Suzzy Kassem

*Some people will only love you as much as they can use you.*
*Their loyalty ends when the benefits stop*

*Sometimes it's not the song that makes you emotional,*
*it's the people and things that come to your mind*
*when you hear it*

*Behind the heart of many strong women lies the memory*
*of a broken little girl that had to learn*
*how to keep getting back up and to never depend on anyone*

— Ravenwolf

*We tend to forget that happiness doesn't come*
*as a result of getting something we don't have,*
*but rather of recognizing and appreciating what we do have*

— Fedrick Hoeneg

*We will always be my love story*

— Ravenwolf

*Stand for your convictions even if you stand alone.*
*Be true to yourself, live your belief*

*Live in every moment you have*
*Destiny waits for no one*

— C. J. Marie

*You become who you think you are.*
*We become what we imagine ourselves to be*

— C. J. Marie

*Your superpower is hope. It inspires us,*
*lifts us up, and never lets you down.*
*It will triumph over any adversity*
*and stand up for whatever our vision is.*
*Hope lies within each of us merely existing*

— C. J. Marie

*I'm stronger because I had to be,*
*I am smarter because of my mistakes,*
*happier because of the sadness.*
*I've known, and now wiser because I learned*

— Gisela Weldon

*I don't have anything to prove to anyone which is a lonely*
*place to be*

— Edward Norton

*If you focus on the hurt, you will continue to suffer.*
*If you focus on the lesson, you will continue to grow*

— Jason Godo

*I lost myself trying to please everyone.*
*Now I am losing everyone while I am finding myself*

*When you dance to your own rhythm,*
*people may not understand you, they may hate you.*
*But mostly they wish they had the courage to do the same*

*She is rare but she is real*

— Mark Anthony

*Love isn't an emotion, it's a frequency*

*You may not control all the events that happen to you, but*
*you can decide not to be reduced by them*

— Maya Angelou

*The only keeper of your happiness is you,
stop giving people power to control your smile, your worth,
and your attitude*

*Never hate jealous people.
They are jealous because they think you are better than them*

*She doesn't settle for less than her soul deserves.
She is brave and beautiful, tender and fierce,
and when she sets her sights on something
she doesn't stop dreaming until it's true*

— Mark Anthony

*A healing friend knows the song in your heart and can hum it
back to you when you have forgotten the melody of life*

— C. J. Marie

*Listen to your inner voice
and not what the world wants you to hear*

— C. J. Marie

*Be aware of those who show they love you,*
*for they may be the one hurting you in disguise*

— C. J. Marie

*Kindness is more than deeds, it is an attitude, an expression,*
*a look, a touch, it is anything that lifts another person*

— C. Neil Strait

*Nothing is more important than empathy for another.*
*Human beings suffering, not a career, not wealth,*
*not intelligence, certainly not status.*
*We have to feel for one another if we are going*
*to survive with dignity*

— Audrey Hepburn

*I want to spend golden time with you, not stolen time*

— C. J. Marie

*Tears weigh nothing, but they carry heavy feelings*

*When we get to the end of our lives together,*
*the houses we had, the cars we drove,*
*the things we possessed won't matter.*
*What will matter is that I had you and you had me*

*Care about what other people think*
*and you will always be their prisoner*

— Leo Tzu

*If you seek peace, be still.*
*If you seek wisdom, be silent.*
*If you seek love, be yourself*

— Becca Lee

*Sometimes the person you'd take a bullet for,*
*may end up being the one behind the gun*

— Tupac Shakur

# Embracing Timeless Beauty

Ageless beauty shines as a beacon for all woman. It is a reflection of the wisdom, energy, and unique essence that everyone possesses within herself. She is courageous, fully in control of her own destiny. She paves the way for empowerment and embodies the true meaning of being a woman of action.

This woman is an influencer, igniting energy and motivation and others to pursue their dreams. She has a vision to inspire good sportsmanship and collaboration. Her wisdom elevates her above the rest, she approaches every moment with an open mind and an ever evolving thoughts, offering creative solutions to the challenges she encounters.

She is a source of hope, connecting with other women to guide them toward the place they were always meant to be even if they hadn't yet realized it. Tenacious and purposeful, she pursues her goals with unwavering determination. She is ageless, limitless, and empowered, living her life with profound intention and purpose.

*She believes in angels and true love*
*and dreams that hold meaning.*
*She is a beautiful flower planted amongst the rocks*
*that bloom not to be seen, but because that's what she does*

— Jon Storm

*Never give someone the opportunity to waste your time*

— Edwin Matos

*It is not your feet that you move.*
*But it is with your heart that you dance*

— Mara

*When nobody wakes you up in the morning,*
*when nobody waits for you at night,*
*and when you could do whatever you want,*
*what do you call it?*
*Freedom or Loneliness*

— Charles Burkowski

*Maybe one day we'll meet again
and explain to each other what really happened*

*There is such beauty in simplicity.
Open your eyes and open your heart and feel God's love*

— C. J. Marie

*I am not perfect, actually I am a perfect imperfection.
I try hard but I make mistakes.
God's love forgives all*

— C. J. Marie

*To be happy you must let go of what's gone,
be grateful for what remains,
look forward to what is coming next.*

*In life you get what you focus on.
So focus on what you want*

*A weak man can't love a strong woman.*
*He won't know what to do with her*

— Alfred Willow

*You deserve somebody who loves to be in your presence*
*and misses you when you are not*

— Mark Anthony

*Find someone who is proud to have you,*
*scared to lose you,*
*fight for you,*
*appreciates you,*
*respects you, cares for you,*
*and loves you unconditionally*

— DEMIC

# *Who are Women of Influence*

They are the ones defining what it means to inspire change, they pave the way for the next generation. They prove with a focused vision, persistence, and resilience a women can accomplish anything. She is a trailblazer of her generation. Age has no limits.

— Unkown

# Life Humbles You

Life humbles you. As you grow older, you stop chasing the big things and start valuing the little things; alone time, enough sleep, a good diet, long walks, and quality time with loved ones. Simplicity becomes the ultimate goal.

– Unknown

*We all dance through the great haul of life,*
*never knowing when the music will fade,*
*yet, one thing is certain...*
*it won't play forever.*
*Every step we take, every twirl we make*
*is singularly never to be repeated.*
*So make each dance meaningful,*
*find joy in the simple movements,*
*be kind, generous, and thoughtful.*
*Let love be the rhythm that guides your every move.*
*Forgive swiftly, love deeply,*
*recognize the impact you leave on the world*
*and those around you.*
*Though the dance might be fleeting*
*it can be filled with grace and purpose.*
*Live each day with passion and ensure your final dance*
*is a celebration of a life beautifully lived.*

– Unknown

*Beauty begins the moment you decide to be yourself*

– Coco Chanel

*Sometimes we desire so deeply to be wanted that we forget the importance of being truly valued and appreciated*

— Morgan Richard Olivier

*Never control him,*
*let him do what he wants so you see what he would rather do.*
*His actions will show you how much he respects you*

*Every woman that finally figured out her wealth,*
*has picked up her suitcases of pride and boarded a flight*
*to freedom which landed in the valley of change*

— Shannon L. Adlen

*When people make remarks about you behind your back,*
*know they are envying you because they lack something they*
*see in you and wish they had.*
*Insecurity screams loudly where confidence is silent*

— C. J. Marie

*No one knows how special she was. She claimed the darkness
of the night, but she was really the star.
She lit the whole place up
leaving her Stardust upon the heads and hearts
of all who were lucky enough to stand beneath her*

– D. G.

*Sometimes I wish I could just rewind back to the old days
with my loved ones and press pause just for a little while*

*May every sunrise bring you hope, and
Every sunset bring you peace*

*You are never too old to set another goal
or dream another dream*

– Leo Brown

*It always seems impossible until it's done*

– Nelson Mendella

*Do you really want to look back at your life
and see how wonderful it could have been
had you not been afraid to live it*

— Carolyn Myss

*Maybe some women are meant to be tamed.
Maybe they need to run free until they find someone
just as wild to run with*

— Sex in the City

*What youth and zest brings to the table,
Age brings wisdom and experience*

— C. J. Marie

*Elegance is the only beauty that never fades*

— Audrey Heburn

*Exist to be happy, not to impress*

*I will never feel sad about getting older.*
*I have confronted life with courage,*
*grace, humility, and strength.*
*Have faced life with a great deal of pride*
*for everything I've been through.*
*I look at the gift of life with peace and gratitude*
*for a life well lived*

\- C. J. Marie

◆

*Each day we live is a victory and a celebration.*
*To travel life's path with inspiration*
*instead of struggle reminds us that life is short*
*and to look at our blessings and appreciate life's goodness*

– C. J. Marie

◆

*At my age I appear older to the young and young to the older.*
*Life has its moments*

◆

*In order to be irreplaceable one must be different*

– Coco Chanel

◆

*Strong women don't play the victim,*
*don't make themselves look pitiful*
*and don't point fingers. They stand and they deal.*
*It's not selfish to love yourself, take care of yourself,*
*and make happiness a priority*

— Mandy Hale

*Don't just be a lady, be a legend*

*With no voice, you are invisble.*
*When your voice is heard, you become empowered*

— C. J. Marie

*I believe that everything happens for a reason.*
*People change so that you can learn to let go,*
*things go wrong so that you appreciate them*
*when they go right, you believe lies so you eventually learn*
*to trust no one but yourself, and sometimes good things*
*fall apart so better things can fall together*

— Marylin Monroe

*In order to be irreplaceable one must be different*

— Coco Chanel

◆

*Live the legacy you want to be remembered by*

— C. J. Marie

◆

*Ageless beauty is the spotlight on all women of all ages.*
*Their individual wisdom cultivate the energy and presence*
*every woman has within herself.*
*She is courageous, bold, and eager to take on any challenge*
*and is in total control of her own life.*
*She is truly an empowered woman*

◆

*True beauty is polished perfection in every way*

— C. J. Marie

◆

*Health is wealth, and wealth is power*

— C. J. Marie

◆

# Thinking Positive

Positive thinking surrounds us, displayed on feel good phrases hung in our homes and splashed across billboards. Yet, despite this encouragement, many people remain consumed by negativity, weighed down by sadness, worry, and anxiety. Positive thinking is more than just a catch phrase It is an emotional and mental attitude that focuses on the goodness in life. It involves managing expectations and thriving for outcomes that promote health, happiness, and success, rather than fixating on fears of anticipating the worst.

# Just the Way You Are

When we are young, we want to look older. When we are old, we want to look younger. There's a window in the middle of it all, when we are supposed to look as we wish. But we waste that time wishing we were taller or thinner or curvier, we wish our hair was longer, shinier, and curlier, and parts of our body were firmer and perkier and so we start to use anti wrinkle cream earlier. Now it's too late to realize that all those things never really mattered in the first place. But it's never too late to start letting go. To want to stop wishing, it's never too late to accept yourself to look in the mirror and realize that all along, you never needed to look older or younger or anything else. You just need to look at you just the way you are.

*Women are a superpower.*
*We are empowered to inspire and to be inspired*

*To get anything good in your life,*
*you have to be ready to sacrifice*

*Call it life-ing, not aging.*
*Chasing youth is futile.*
*All we can do is embrace who we are at the moment we are in,*
*and be okay*

— Pamala Anderson

*Someone will always be prettier,*
*Someone will always be smarter,*
*Someone will always be younger.*
*But they will never be you*

— Freddie Mercury

*The worst feeling isn't being lonely, it's being forgotten*

◆

*There is no better feeling than knowing you help someone be a better version of themselves*

— C. J. Marie

◆

*Once the heart gets heavy with pain, people don't cry, they just turn silent... Completely silent*

◆

*Forgiving is not forgetting, forgiving is remembering without pain*

— Ceclia Cruz

◆

*When opportunity presents itself, grab it, hold tight and don't let go*

◆

*We can't always choose the music life plays for us, but we can choose how we dance to it*

◆

*A beautiful face will age, a perfect body will change,*
*but a beautiful soul will always be beautiful*

*Always remember that the life in front of you*
*is more important than the life behind you*

*I truly believe my sole purpose is to help empower,*
*inspire, and motivate others to unlock their fullest potential*
*and live their best life*

— Roxie Nafousi

*Life doesn't always get better, but you do.*
*You get stronger, you get wiser, you get softer,*
*with target wings you rise.*
*The world watches all in wonder,*
*at the breathless beauty of a human who survived life*

*If you can't do anything about it, then let it go.*
*Don't be a prisoner to the things you can't change*

*You have to dance like there's nobody watching,*
*Love like you'll never be hurt,*
*Sing like there's nobody listening, and*

*Live like it's heaven on earth*

— Carmen Rosa Murguetio Romo

◆

*I'm not afraid of being alone wolf,*
*I choose to go solo, honor my instincts,*
*and follow the beat of my heart*

◆

*The universe is saying to you today,*
*don't block what's coming by doubting if it's even possible.*
*Worry and lack of trust only slows down the process.*
*Your turnaround is going to happen quickly,*
*trust yourself, everything is possible*

◆

*In the end people will judge you anyway,*
*so don't live your life impressing others,*
*live your life impressing yourself*

*Solitude is dangerous, it's addictive.*
*Once you see how peaceful it is*
*you don't want to deal with people*

*My face may have wrinkles,*
*but I won't let anything wrinkle my heart*

– C. J. Marie

*Age wrinkles the body,*
*quitting wrinkles the soul,*
*instead of aging think of it as life-ing*

*Don't make excuses to execute ideas*

– C. J. Marie

*When a woman sees a beautiful 25 year old*
*we think back to the days of our youth.*
*What our age brings to the table is wisdom and experience*

— C. J. Marie

*Women are survivors,*
*they are the great warriors of aging with all our wrinkles,*
*grey hair, and extra pounds,*
*age is like fine wine*

— C. J. Marie

# *Empty Nest*

Few people truly discuss the emotions that arise when your children leave home to start their own lives. A bittersweet loneliness often takes hold as you face the reality of an empty nest and begin the journey of rediscovering yourself. Motherhood is a lifelong commitment, and even as you watch your children spread their wings and follow their own paths, the sense of loss can feel overwhelming. Yet, deep down, we understand that letting them go is a necessary part of their growth.

Now, it's their turn to live, learn, and create their own stories. As mothers, we stand silently on the sidelines, watching with pride and a hopeful heart, always cheering them on from afar.

# *The Truth About Aging*

D on't let anyone tell you that aging is just a number, it's only a number if you choose to see it that way. Your body, however, tells a different story. There isn't an elderly woman who wakes up in the morning, looks in the mirror, and doesn't wonder, *where did the young person I once was go?*

One thing is certain: mirrors don't lie. Whether we want to admit it or not, time leaves its mark. These changes are irreversible unless you go under the knife or resort to facial fillers. Every wrinkle, sagging bit of skin, arthritic finger, graying hair, and shifting posture is a testament to the passage of time. Even our teeth seem to spread, our eyesight weakens, and weight becomes an ongoing battle. If that weren't enough, we also become more vulnerable to disease. This stark reality serves as a reminder that youth is fleeting and will never return. From the tops of our heads to the tips of our toes, everything changes.

The cosmetic industry thrives on this inevitability, generating billions of dollars by selling the promise of restored youth. But we cannot deny the truth of aging—our physical youth is gone. However, if we cultivate a positive attitude toward aging, we won't fight it; instead, we will appreciate the privilege of growing older. After all, many never get that chance.

True beauty never fades because it radiates from within. Aging brings its own unique beauty—the beauty of freedom. As we grow older, we care less about what others think, allowing us to embrace the courage and wisdom that only time can provide. It's true that time has passed us by, and we will never be exactly as we once were, nor will we do the things we could only do in our youth. But self-acceptance is the key to inner beauty.

There will be moments of nostalgia when we see a young woman and think, *I once looked like that too.* But if she is lucky enough to reach old age, she will also discover the freedom and wisdom that come with it. Life is the best game in town, and we should play it to the fullest. We cannot stop time or the changes it brings, but we can choose to make the best of it. No matter what the mirror reflects, we know how to live—and that is the greatest gift of all.

I believe the best is yet to come, with no boundaries or limitations. Age will never hold me back from achieving my goals.

# Celebrate Your Age

Even if our bodies are no longer what they once were, they carry our souls, our courage, and our strength. We should enter this chapter of our lives with humility, grace, elegance, and pride, embracing everything we have experienced throughout our lifetime. Growing older should never be a source of regret or sadness. Instead we must remember that aging is a privilege denied to many.

It's time to celebrate age, it's never too late to sparkle and shine. The years may sneak up on us, passing by before we even realize it. But defying age means looking inward and embracing our inner beauty. While our beauty is fleeting, inner beauty endures for a lifetime. So yes, I have aged, but I welcome new beginnings. I celebrate the woman I am today, standing boldly and proudly, with the hopeful belief that 'the best is yet to come,' all while wearing a positive smile.

# Don't Count the Years

Don't count the years, my love, they do not show the quality of how your life is spent. Don't place false value on what mirrors know, the beauty love reflects is truer meant. Don't long for youthful times that used to be or mourn dreams that never did come true. The past is the best used as a memory. Every day can build new dreams for you. Don't thrust aside the honor of your age, nor make acceptance difficult and glum. Relentless ticks of the clock, despite your rage. So live with pride in what you have become. Dear heart, the love that fills our life so much creates a magic age that time can't touch.

– Unknown

# Conclusion

My hope is that this book of quotes and reflections inspires you on your journey towards self revelation. Quotes have a unique way of resonating with us, offering insights that become profoundly meaningful when we apply them to our own lives. My vision is that all women, everywhere, find the courage to live their truth, embracing their authentic beauty, wisdom, and strength. May these qualities light the path to honoring and celebrating the extraordinary woman you are destined to become.

*Your time on earth is limited.*
*Don't try to age with grace:*
*Age with mischef, audacity,*
*and a good story to tell.*

— Mel Greenberg

# Author's Note

As we age, the natural and inevitable changes to our body and mind will unfold. Ultimately, it comes down to your attitude towards growing older. While external beauty may fade, inner beauty endures for a lifetime. Kindness, compassion, and empathy are the true essence of inner beauty.

Thinking of age as life-ing — an opportunity to embrace the perfection of each passing year and to recognize the blessings we have received. Take the time to connect with your inner self and discover the wisdom within. Let the quotes in this book inspire you to see that true beauty is ageless, rooted in your perception of yourself.

Outer beauty may catch the eye, but it is the inner self that truly matters. Never surrender your power. As Eleanor Roosevelt so eloquently stated, "no one can make you feel inferior without your consent." Believe in yourself, because if you don't, no one else will. Own your confidence, embody your strength, and step into the world as the elegant and extraordinary woman you are.

# About the Author

C.J. is the author of many inspirational books. An educator by profession, she has received numerous awards for her writing achievements. She is featured in Who's Who Among American Teachers and, as an entrepreneur, she was honored with the International and Business Career Award, C.J. has been recognized by the New York Assembly with a "Woman of Distinction" citation, as well as being selected as one of The Empowered Women of Queens, New York.

C.J. is a certified life coach and a personal consultant specializing in pageantry. As a multi-time, state and national queen, herself, she understands the importance of style and fostering a positive self-image. With over forty years of experience in the pageant arena, C.J. brings a wealth of knowledge and expertise to her work.

Beyond her professional accomplishments, C.J. is deeply involved in her community. She participates in bereavement groups, offering support to those dealing with grief. As a philanthropist, she devotes her time, talents, and resources to various charitable causes. Her artwork has been used to raise funds for churches and events, and she has donated proceeds from her book sales to those in need.

C.J's mission is rooted in service, bringing smiles, hope, and joy to those who need it most. She firmly believes that life's greatest rewards come from giving to others. For her, the most meaningful accomplishments transcend financial success and lie in the positive impact made on the lives of others.

www.ingramcontent.com/pod-product-compliance
Lightning Source LLC
Chambersburg PA
CBHW050905120626
46554CB00003B/1021